MW01609116

Without Wings

by

Erin Zarro

DEDICATION

For all the men who have changed my life just by having known them and loving them; for my husband, who now holds my heart.

For every woman out there who's loved and lost; for every woman who's survived an abusive relationship.

In loving memory of my grandfather, James E. Conroy, whose love for my grandmother knew no boundaries. Whose love taught me how to love and be loved. I love you, Gramps.

THE OPERA OF CIRCUMSTANCE

If I could erase the blackboard that is my mind
If I could erase your sweet candy words
        and your love-whispers
if I could erase the connection
I felt
        when I looked into your eyes...
that's when the dawn-light shone down on me
and brushed away the darkness.

Happiness was finding you,
the one whose soul is twin to mine,
we're two halves of the same circle,
always connected,
one heartbeat echoing the other,
like a synchronized orchestra –
in love-rhythms we played;
in love-rhythms we died –
prematurely, never missing a beat,
to the opera of circumstance.

Now that our spring-love has ended
and a winter of death is here,
I want to erase it all:
erase my feelings;
wipe them clean,
erase dream visions of you,
sever them from my mind;
erase our passion-music,
let every love-note disappear into night.

My heart is as cold as the frost of winter
an icy wind of memories surrounds me –
enveloping me in its blanket devoid
of feeling and warmth –

I still see you in shadows.
In the blizzard-winds, somewhere
I hear you whisper my name.

And I am afraid –
to feel, to love, to live again,
to remember
you

to be as cold as death itself
  to be as cold as the winter –

LOVE LETTERS

1.
We're like the 5 of Cups,
love spilled from Niagara sunsets.
You were made of dreams to me.

Under moonlight,
you pressed my wishes into night,
and gave me the stars on bended knee.

I look for you in those sunsets,
rainbows hidden in your eyes
holding hope for a simpler existence.

You studied Wagner and Bach,
and French fell out of you like poetry.

Your darkroom was our special place
where we stopped time
as we captured images in its fire-red glow –
Our hands moved in slow rhythms
until I became your angel,
the perfect girl at age 19.

How I wish I could still be her to you;
April wedding white,
filled with eggshell promises,
looking at you with newlywed eyes.

2.
I saw our demise in fallen stars,
your orchestrated distance,
anger reaching past sullen letters.
How I still feel your touch,
winter-cold and shattered like glass,

how freedom speaks in tentative syllables
as I listen to Pink Floyd,
and want to be tangled up with you
in perpetual dance.

And how I still see you in the darkroom,
watching me with transparent eyes.

You're a whisper of memory now
faded into dreams
and I your fallen angel.

ANATOMY OF DIVORCE

An arrow slammed into my heart
the day you told me
you no longer loved me or wanted
to spend your life with me as promised
no amount of painkillers could end
this ceaseless, all-consuming pain I feel.

My entire world fell away and all that existed was pain
You live deep inside my heart
I couldn't remove you if I tried—I end
where you begin; our souls are intertwined.

You fell out of love with me –
we're slowly suffocating together.
This mechanical, artificial thing called life
drags on without the promise

Of love, of meaning...without you, without my heart.
I never wanted to lose you –
to feel you pull away, leave me wanting;
looking into your eyes and seeing your betrayal,
the pain writhing inside, reflected back to me

like a nightmare that traps me –
I lay screaming and sweating and awake.
You promised me a lifetime, 120 years.
Instead, you tore my heart out of my chest,
still beating, bleeding.
You left me cold, forgotten, inside a tomb I can't see or feel.
I'm alone.
My world ended softly, inconsequential.
Our love, seemingly endless,
you left to die, mutilated, rotting as it never should have.
I will always want you in a deep part of me.

The flame still flickers as time waltzes on, unaware
While you still bring me pain

instead of roses.
You bring me numbness, yet my heart
still beats strong.
But it can't bring you back to me;
nor wipe away the bad.
It can't promise me the eternity we could have had,
make promises of marriage.
It can't change our path. But it ends
as surely as the night dissolves away, as surely as my heart
still bleeds. There is nothing I want more
than to sever the connection, all those parts of you
that connected us together.
End the pain

of losing you more each day, time sliding from my fingers.
Of losing the part of you that changed me, gave me hope.
That evolved under your tender wing.
Broken promises line our path, promises
that I held in my heart. My hope is gone, obliterated;
I can't endure the pain

of us dying, fading away, missing you beyond the end –
this finality of hearts and words.
I don't want to say goodbye, to let our love die.
Our hearts go on, somehow, broken and bereft.
Hearts mourning and bleeding and fighting
the split in our paths that will take us
in new directions, new places, alone.

Nothing changes. Nothing moves. We've reached the end.
Embrace what we were, and let us go.

Still, you are inside me
even though we've reached the end of our time together,
still, your promises hurt like open wounds,
still you are infinite pain to me,
yet you still live inside my heart,
deep where forgotten dreams go,
and where love rests in peace.

SINGULAR

It's the little things —

an empty bed where you should be,
the mattress molded to our two forms
as we slept entangled as one,
an unending line from your body to mine;
Your heart never far, beating so close to mine, so close –

It becomes a singular heartbeat.

How I turn over and expect to see you and you aren't there —

a ghost of what was
leaving footprints in my mind;
in my heart.

How I faced the wall, squeezed my eyes shut, and imagined —

I was back home with you,
the night table on one side,
fingers of moonlight reaching down
to illuminate the room.

How if I wished it hard enough,
I could still feel you beside me
once again, your warmth,
the in and out motion of your breath.

How you would curl around me even in your sleep,
an angel caught in earthbound repose.

How you'd smile as you greeted me from a long day at work —

How it chased away the bad,
how nothing seemed more important than you in that
singular moment when everything else dissolved away.

I see that special smile every night in my dreams,
how it still lights up the shadows in my mind.

A bullet could not hurt as much as losing you, how you left me
all alone, shattered into pieces –

How I lost a part of myself,
How you will carry it with you forever.

I want to banish you from my mind, make it as if we never were.
I want to erase everything you've said,
those whispers and laughs and smiles;
all those nights you held me as I drifted off to
sleep.

How you became the rainbow after my storm of life,
how I knew you'd always be there after the rain.

On this day, I wish to go where I've never been –
cast off the past seven years,

Lay myself bare – walk alone –

How I'm just me, as I was before you,
how I've changed after living a lifetime
with you, how I will now be

Singular –

(Without you).

FLY AWAY
To Abby - an inspiration

Cast off yer chains, woman
Cast off that which doesn't belong
        shed old expectations like rotten skin
useless and failing.

Cast off yer attitude, woman
        Yer world view - *two become one*—
but not so.

It's time you fly alone
        time to stretch yer wings heavenward
take flight - leap - towards yer future
        yer new life.

Cast off yer old life, woman
compromise - duality - turmoil –
        Love. Love that sustained you
A treasured memory - a slice of life - entanglement of
        two hearts, two souls.

Shed them - bleed - chin up —
        Fly away.

ALONE AGAIN

I shed my old self with your ring.

I spent many nights alone
walking on walls of myself
crawling through memories
listening to every heartbeat
knowing that if I could survive one,
I could survive them all.

Nights passed by like
lazy clouds.

I packed up your smiles, your gifts and your love
knowing that even though there'd be no
physical evidence
in the darkroom's red glow
I would still see you
mouthing wishes and advice.
Perhaps even love –

I locked the door of memories on us
and tried to unremember
 – undo, unlove, unlearn – you.
How to forget someone who has changed my life?
How to wipe my life clean;
make it sterile, white.

I walked toward an unknown destination
becoming someone I had yet to meet.

Alone.

AFTER

You've burrowed yourself into my heart and
taken up residence—
You're as much a part of me as my own heart,
the constant beating, the sound of life that resounds
within thin walls.

You're as much a part of me as my soul –
how we've intertwined our separate lives
together; a thing greater than the sum of its parts.

We wove each other into the fabric
of our lives, so much that the threads blur and tangle,
and there is no way to tell one from
another. They're merged; identical, not two but one.

That doesn't speak of what we've endured
a storm of deception that threatens to pour down on us
at any moment;
learning to speak the delicate language of marriage,
of compromise, of faith.

Faith that can lend light to any darkness we stumble upon;
a fierce knowing, a truth.

We've walked over our own flames, burning us to the core,
but we held on to each other, and made it to the other side.

We survived.

As one, we can fight anything that life tosses our way.
We can light the dark; fill ourselves up with it.

Together, as one, we can do anything.

So after the storm, after the heartbreak and tears and broken
promises,

I have to ask you: is there something worth saving,
worth fighting for?

Is there light somewhere in that blackness of anger, of death?
Is there a measure of hope within all that loss?
Is there a blip of life inside all the death?

Please shine the light, find the path – don't let us die.
You were the best of me, the heart of me, the other half of me.

You will always have a place inside my heart, *your place*,
after the clouds part and the sun shines again.

After it's over, after the new, after us.

WITHOUT YOU

Night embraces us
Love holds us
this memory
that whispers in my ear
and wraps itself around my dreams –
this lonely sleep,
this desolate waking
is because of you.

Cold heart,
sad eyes
melancholy dream.

This tear,
this burning
this pain
is me without you.

Night laughs at me,
dreams deceive.
The moon hides you.
Shadows dance on walls
and sometimes I think you are
one of them
always moving, always masked.

The way you slip into the night,
walk through my dreams and depart
as quickly, fading like a rainbow
in the mist.

Every day I search for your traces –
your footsteps upon my soul:
I seek your path when it converges

into mine
and we become part of each other,
a blending of life, of love.

So close there's no end
to how our skin and spirits weave themselves
together
and soar.

I reach for you
in my dreams
and pull myself through another darkened day
without you.

Movements haunt me,
your spirit calls to me,
and I grow tired of living
without your embrace.

The silence is cold
it tears through my heart
and burns through every piece of me –
everything I am, everything I will be,
without you.

LIKE CANDY

You lay there, tears wet on your face,
and told me your truth:

things that shattered me like glass.

I see myself reflected in those jigsaw images –
a phantom of what was,
of what may never be.

A future that dissolved before my very feet
into the cold loneliness of living
without you, without your heart beating against my own,
without your hands, precious gifts, to hold me.

You filled me up with fuzzy warm feel-good lies—
illusions, every one.
Illusions plucked from your deepest desires
and held out to me to examine, make some sense
of the twisted place inside your head.

The pathology of it is clear:

a connection has been broken, bleeding.
Something is missing within your eyes –
they no longer speak to me.

There's a problem in need of diagnosis and treatment,
little things erode at the core.
Little things that fall away every day, every hour.

You won't acknowledge anything –
ignorance is a beautiful bliss
Choice is overrated, and so is honesty.

You aren't the person you once were long ago,
with a big heart and whispered promises
of love and a future.
On bended knee, you told me your truth:
and thus began the war.

The war within you that wouldn't cease;
a war you weren't strong enough to fight.
Instead you left me ignorant and happy,
made me believe in your delusions,
made me cling to them
when all was lost, and shattered everything I held dear,
everything I believed with my whole heart.
And thus blew my world to bits, scattered pieces, remains.

Lost forever.

It's all part of the fantasy world you created,
the walls you've placed around yourself,
around your heart,
always on guard.

Unmovable, untouchable, you exist only in shadows.
And I can't reach you –
you are too far away. You're a landmine,
built to destroy everything you touch.
The chasm between us grows wider.
I reach out with tentative hands and grasp only air;
only lies.

Your truth is poison
that burns everything it touches.
You can kill with a single glance;
evasion, evasion, evasion.
Still you choose to stuff it down –
believe, believe, believe.
Still you choose to surrender to the poison,

and die slowly, day after day,
a ghost man walking.

My truth – the light that illuminates —
that eclipses the dark— will set you free,
set you on the path of right, of love. Of freedom.

My truth goes down clear and easy, like candy.

before breathing

frozen :
in a sea of silence
dead :
before you can breathe
        before your heart starts beating
floating among metaphors
        to numb the pain

I can live without him.
I can live without him.

Stuck in dark places
you didn't mean to go
demons swimming on the surface
of your brain
stained by
anger,
scarred with tears

I can live without him.
I can live without him.

pain :
an exposed wound,
leaking blood, leaking rotting love
stitched and sterilized
before
infection

(loneliness infects a broken heart)

there is no exit, no cure
for this condition –

I can live. without .

YOUR SILENCE IS MY FOREVER

It was lost forever
in December frost
a perfect dream
tossed out the window
of possibility.
I shiver inside your silence.

I breathe in your words that
float in silence

It's a long journey to forever
without you. Without the possibility
of your touch, your laughter
the way your eyes freeze,

rivet on mine. Hungry stares. Your eyes windows.
You stand between two dreams
and one, one faraway dream
has to die. Left to rot of its own silence
ripped through the night sky, a dream
lost to us forever.

In December frost,
you love me. It was one of many possibilities
played amongst our shadowed nights, impossible
to ignore. Our dreamworld.
Your face frozen
melted by time ticking silent
we felt forever
in quicksand hearts and eyes, piercing windows

to our inner selves, windows
that let us be who we really are, the possible
pain erased. Painted with each kiss, forever

caught in a dream
held in moonlight, carried silently
into December's frost.

What shattered was the window,
the connection cut. It was impossible
to reach you. You were no longer mine.
Forever is only a dream
I hold in my hand,
drifting silently to its grave
along with December's frost.

Alone in my own frost-world
the world shivers outside my window.
He is the silence
I wear, the possibilities and dreams
I carry. Cast into moon's light,
they are gone forever.

In December frost we loved as in a dream
Cast out the window of possibles
Your silence is my forever.

PIECES OF YOU (AFTER DECEMBER)

I dreamt of you, after December.
I swore I'd always love you, after December.

The stars stare at me with your eyes
and haunt my nights, after December.

I drift through life, alone and formless
and love you as I swore, after December.

We meet in twilight dreams
so I can love you again, after December.

Shadows form our shape. Our voices push though the darkness.
I pray for your return, after December.

I crawl through the streets whispering your name
I hunger for your touch, after December.

I live the life of a half moon, incomplete and bleeding.
I call your name, after December.

I search the cosmos and in every dream
and find pieces of you, after December.

INSIGNIFICANT

I was insignificant, a speck of dust
in your universe.
I was the enemy, even though I presented myself
without defenses:
I had none –
no barriers between me and your rejection.
You didn't care –
I was part of your life, but I wasn't *in* it. Not really.
I was a statue standing tall with no voice, a glass figurine
to look at and admire
But when the glass shattered and I spoke my truth,
I ceased to exist.

Insignificant.

I wasn't a person to you I was an object I wasn't allowed
to feel. To speak. To be heard. I was nothing.
Numb and grieving,
I walked alone.

You were no comfort, no sanctuary for my soul.
The house still bears echoes of us; of my suffering.
Sometimes, in my dreams, I still see you,
your eyes filled with rage –

I still hear your angry words, feel them like blades
on my skin – ripping, tearing, obliterating.
I was without defenses, without hope to hold me.

You didn't understand. You *wouldn't* understand.
It hung there, between us, a glass wall.
We could see each other, but couldn't touch.
When I reached for you,
you were no longer there.

But I was less than pristine, damningly flawed –

Insignificant, a shadow to myself.

RAINFALL

Memories of you come as unrelenting
as the rainfall.

They speak with your tongue
and surround my body in rainfall.

My heart aches incomplete
and burns as fire unaffected by rainfall.

I lie in the air of leaving
and whisper your name into rainfall.

Every shadow bears your shape.
I crawl through darkness praying for rainfall.

I soak my soul into you
as I give in to your rainfall.

OUT & THROUGH THE FORGETTING

Forgetting is what's hard to do.
The memories attack me
when I'm not ready to feel them:
T-Birds dancing in my mind,
with you at the wheel,
an '80s metal tape
played and replayed
with you singing along;
forbidden kisses stolen at midnight.
Losing you in the cold of winter,
my heart will always be
frozen in yesterday.
That's when I think of you
when it's cold with death outside,
the death of love,
the death of us.
I wish the memories would melt like ice
and disappear,
so I could forget,
so I would stop loving you.
That's when great poems are written –
when you can't erase the pain
and memories clog your mind;
'the only way out is through', Frost said.
This is my way through.
Maybe someday I'll walk out to a winter day
and not think of you.

HEART OF STONE

I think you must have a heart of stone.
You guard it day after day, impenetrable, alone.
Air is thick and I can't get through.
You must be a statue, unmovable you.

You stand guard, a face of stone.
I sit in stilled silence untouched and alone.
You must be a statue, unmovable you.
Our love, wrapped in ice, turns blue.

I sit in stilled silence untouched by you.
Days grow long and my heart hardens with you.
Our neglected love shivers alone.
We stand together, made of stone.

Days grow old and my heart hardens with you
Our love dies slowly and then fades from view.
We stand together, still made of stone.
Marriage should not be left to die alone.

Our love dies slowly and fades from view.
We waste away in our darkened tomb
Marriage should not be left to die alone.
We weren't meant to die this way, in stone.

We waste away in our own tomb
Years pass and I still can't reach you.
We weren't meant to die alone.
Our marriage is preserved forever, cast in stone.

TANGLED

Eight years tore open that night –
the night you followed me
with your eyes.

You're a paradox – breathing monosyllables,
but somehow, I held your attention –
in my hand, fingering rough edges,
melancholy eyes, thoughts trapped beneath
your stark silence –
I touched it as if to touch you –
explore the landscape of your skin,
the fabric of memory;
peel you apart and wrap you around me
like silk.

I'm the one with fire-eyes,
a connection, an answer to the whispers
of your soul.

Your eyes, how they reveal so much –
what's buried in past lives,
what still tangles you. Slowly,
from the voice that keeps you
bewitched, from the light that still
dances in your eyes, the same eyes that
held me so long ago.

You say you don't want me,
but it's your eyes
that speak a different language.

And how I wish I could look through you,
through paper-thin lies,
and not answer.

WINDOWS

Night hides you from my eyes
and shadows melt into twilight dreams.

We are parasols perched on the
transparency of day.
We can't pull ourselves out of form,
erase illusions.
Your words seep into my skin,
my thoughts chase your footsteps
in stilled silence.

We quiver on the edge
of balance,
with only words to rise between us,
displaced smiles.

Yet we fall into
the liquid of past, whispers of regret.
Night is hollow, reaching out with heavy hands.
I feel the chill of abandonment,
drowning in unanswered questions,
my eyes catch on shadows,
begging them to be you.

I become just another blank face,
with windows for eyes,
shattered mirrors,
jagged, incomplete,
the truth cutting through me
like glass.

BLEEDING STARS

Dreams settle into shadows
as we cling to each other –

Our time is finite
damp with absence,
a wish thrown into sunset.
How I want to see you,
as you rise from mundane hours
and find me,
trapped in the satin of sky,
holding starlight promises.

We steal small eternities –
the pieces of existence
we can't mold into words,
the shape of regret.

Love is only a memento
plucked from our somber nights
and pressed into memory.
It haunts us in our dreams;
it whispers through dark spaces.

Eyes like pendulums,
we're dancing shadows,
bleeding stars.

WORDS LIKE CHAINS

Night is a black hole,
and reveals nothing
through lightning-cracks in clouds,
iced moonlight.

As we lie, embraced,
our bodies puzzle pieces,
I feel you shift behind me,
your skin touching me like
the breath of summer,
your heartbeat like sad drums.

We were a dream, once –
but now dissolve
into sterile light,
love wiped away like dust.

I watch you with lucid eyes, and wait –

I've held no illusions, just love
in my hands, fluttering like butterflies
that land on your body, wanting nourishment.

But you no longer sustain me.
You regard me with keyhole eyes,
expectations spilling out of every breath.
You are empty silence, love unraveled from
cold places.

I cannot be anyone except who I am,
with famished heartbeats
and a fragmented existence.
I wear your words like chains,
binding me to tomorrow,

heavy footsteps.
Your anger spreads through me
like fire. It fills me with
smoke-filled words, your hands flames.

I reach for you but you aren't there.
You've faded into twilight
and dance with the stars.
You've left me with only the memory
of where you lay
to sustain me,
and the smell of death
everywhere you've touched.

this is not a love poem

stilted conversation
early in the a.m.
i awaken to the butterflies
in my stomach
and a soulful prayer
that this time
i'll get through to you
this time –

fear
about what you'll say
or not say
your thoughts
are a mystery waiting
to be unraveled –

the muted emotions
hang over us,
ready to crash down on us
anytime
exploding in our faces
and then it'll be out there –

our naked emotions
revealed to the world.

the world's heart stops beating
as the butterflies
tiptoe around the silence
as i reach for the perfect words
that mean something
to you
anything that moves you
from this icicle of emotion

you're trapped in.
i'll wait till the right time
to love you –

someday you will want me –
all I have are wishing-star memories
and stilted nervous conversation
in the morning
unspoken thoughts burn in our minds
simmer through the silence
and nowhere to go
to get away from it all
except to each other.

but instead
you tossed me out of your life,
leaving only a memory –

those who can't see the truth are the ones
who have lost their vision.

THE ART OF DISSOCIATION

I emerge
out of myself
from a cocoon
of lost visions.
I hold shadows
of faded nightmares
sleeping metamorphosis –

dissociation, it is.
To master the art,
I must purge you from me,
        shed your memories like dead skin,
        cut you out of my heart.
My heart, swaddled in bandages, must heal.
Then, you will be removed.

Removed
from this trembling mass
of *me*

devastated
by your shutter-click exit
left me slithering
in shadows
that were us.

Crawling through life
with the light bulb broke
and no map to guide me home.

No directions, no safety net, no
dress rehearsal.

This is it, the Big Show
watch me emerge from livid sleep
and crawl towards light.

Your words breathe
        out of my skin
as darkness sinks in –

CATHARSIS

This poem sings to me
       in the shower, in a high soprano
as water drips lazily down my body
       cleansing every bit of filth
from the day.

Sometimes I hear the wind
       whisper my name;
sometimes I think it's you

Better not give me the key
       to unlock your dreams –
I'll slip into your subconscious,

with my dark gray-cloud eyes and a ghost-smile
       cutting into your dreamland
with surgical precision
(just as he did
       4 years prior and I still feel his
touch of ice-cold love on my lips)

Listen to my every word,
watch as images assault your helpless body
       you can't stop the movie playback
       is my payback
Don't listen to the sound
       of my heart as it snaps in two
and I bleed rotted love on the floor.

AFTERMATH

I didn't tell him
that June night
as we wrapped ourselves up
in each other –

as his skin fused with my skin
my head tucked
    between his head
and his heart

that I cried.

I cried
my breath drawing in breath
voodoo crazy
whispering shattered pleas
to just make it

stop.

Wipe my pain away, paintbrush in hand;
draw me painless and forgetful.

Forgetful tear-catcher
praying upon a shooting star
that all nights don't fall
into
this

I didn't tell him
that although we were soclose

I stood behind glass apologies
my heart behind bars –

SPOONFED

You said I'd be the first to know
when your fairy tale-life exploded
        in your face

I sit by the phone
waiting
to be fed your words
        through the phone line
yet the phone sits mute

and my thoughts
        are wrapped in you.

My soul, famished,
can't be satisfied –
this heart-hunger keeps calling.

You ripped me open
        and watched me bleed;

I bled loving words and pleas
but you turned winter-cold
        and marched away

to fight your heart.

Words unspoken –
a waterfall of past moments
soaking me mindless
in this silence
of hearts unbeat

and nights unlived.

You are a love song
folded into a tightly wrapped package
tossed into time

while visions –

(kisses melted into moonlight
smiles stolen and eyes seduced;
December endings –)

remain;

a coiled phone cord
feeding me

your silence.

MIXED SIGNALS

Your kind of love
 is an oxymoron.

Our connection is a
downed phone line,

severed and barely breathing –

oh please pull the plug
Love is brain dead.

In the night your desire
perfumes the air;

our hearts began this
dance of passion.
It's mind-numbing, mind-boggling
and acrobatic. Nitrous eyes –
mind full of moonlight –
bodies dripping

In the morning I'm cold –
my heart on ice

my body your living cadaver.

CHILL.

My heart
lies on your altar
        of sacrifice
frozen –

ice-eyes stare through me.

I dwell
in stagnant air
of leaving.

We're music
that floats through
December-soaked breezes.

Wrapped in high school forevers
        and pounding hearts

We found it –
our version of love.

I held it
those death-cold nights
with your promises
chained to my heart.

We lost it –
my days were hazy and formless.

I dwelled in the Chill
of your silence.

Your promises seep into my mind,
leaving little droplets
shattered words,
frozen heart –

Snowflakes are memories
blowing around me
the connection severed
like fallen icicles.

EXAMINATION

Fingers probe
wilted flesh
explore topography
of emotion

thoughts
sliced open –

I'd never seen you cry until then.
Your shrouded feelings
left me feeling cold
sitting on the examination table
waiting –

You snapped shut
your mouth bloated
with words
hammering through flesh –

Feelings boxed up
sit with the garbage –
marked "fragile"

at night
under gangrene stars
I hear them
tiptoe through the house
        misplaced souls,
the shrapnel of life.

we listen to
tentative beats
        of butterfly hearts

we stand there
looking through each other
mismatched lines tangled
unfilled and unshaded
a work in progress –

PERMANENCE

We stand by the door
like children
daring each other
to step forward
on wounded legs
cast faded moments
into spring breezes

In your words
your love-dreams
open the door
to us

as sands tumble
through the hourglass,
visions are painted
on the walls
of memory

I count the days
as they grow old

I count
how many times I've
looked in the mirror
and didn't see you

I don't have hands to hold you
or lips to kiss you

I can't hold on to
precious seconds,
minutes as they

fall through
my fingers

I reach for you
and hope you are
reaching for me, too.

Your words embed themselves
in my mind,
seal themselves
into my soul

such permanence
I carry
forever

PHONE CALL

It's an addiction, this phone call thing.
Every day creeps by until
the hour when phone lines connect us.

Every day we talk,
but I can't seem to break through
the wall you've built around your heart,
every day it feels like I'm losing you
in a sea of distance.

A daily phone call equals love
in my equation of life,
but your math skills don't add up.
You and I both know the truth,
the truth that whispers in our ears
during our transparent conversations,
the truth that I'm just not ready
to believe

You laugh, talk about nothing
and leave me dangling
listening
to the dial tone
that annoying buzz
always reminding me
that you are
not mine.

SKIN

See me without skin
without preconceptions or edges
to define.
Peel layers off my skin, as I am,
see underneath, down to my soul,
see the light that makes me.

I am not perfect, but this is me.
Nothing to disguise bumps and bulges,
wrapped as I am, naked in my skin
I have a beautiful soul, you said.
With nothing to dull the sharp edges
of a heart broken, love lost.
I am an enigma, tough to define.

If you try to define
what makes me
shade in the boundaries, scrutinize each cell.
I am your specimen.
To love me you must
know everything –
blotchy skin, gray nearsighted eyes,
rounded edges, lack of grace, balance.
Peer into my soul

And see, really see, who I am,
my soul is your soul.
There is no way to define
our edges –
You. Me. Us.
Become each other's skin
human imperfection is heavenly perfection. I am

your wife. I am
yours. You see me in this human-skin
We are linked together, our souls
merged; undefined.
You love me
with my sharp edges

your soul linked with mine to its outer edges
You know it to the tips of your toes, that I am
the one. You know me
and chose me, the one who fits your soul
like one half of a full moon.
A phenomenon undefined.
You love me in this skin.

You know my sharp edges and soul
yet still love me
as I am, not defined
perhaps only misunderstood.
You still love me
in every way I am
in my skin.

CRUSHED

My dreams are thick with rain,
and I don't know where you
reside
in the vast confusion of my mind,
eyes filled with clouds
ears filled with thunder.

Standing on the edge
of a moment,
I look within us
and see days shatter,
the pieces sit on the floor
surrounded by dead words
spread-eagled in rigor mortis.

Crystalline promises wash away
with the downpour, dreams freeze
with the chill.
Eyes turn transparent and useless.

We sit inches apart
but there's a hundred years
between us,
days grow heavy with soured speech
and delusions.

Weeks pass by like cloudy visions,
we don't move from the silence.

We're consumed by it,
with prayers thrown into night.
It's dark and I can't see you.
I can't be you,
walk inside your mind,

fingers probing thoughts,
feet moving through dreams.

I wear torn wishes and anger.
I don't know where to reach you

in this empty place without a name
or location,
with a faceless demon
sucking the love from us,
its sustenance.

No place to go from here.
I've sewn my life shut
and gasp for precious air.

We become the silence.

Soon, its weight will
crush us.

GUILTY FOR LOVING YOU

Night is a void, hollowed out and starless.
Not a whisper of emotion, or prayer.
My voice is lost with the dreams
that held me.

Your face takes shape
in night's darkness,
only a vision –
thoughts probe the night
for answers.

We're in a place not easily defined.
Words are shrouded in riddles, in rhyme,
plastic smiles and untruths.

We're wingless birds seeking shelter
from the chill
yet there is no shelter.
Just laughter sealed in tears.

Shadows coat each wall and dance
at night. Broken dreams hide in mirrors,
reflect the truth,
the starless existence that we don't want to face.

If I look far enough,
maybe I'll see the future.
Maybe I'll see my broken self
staring me in the eyes, asking why.
My eyes are as blank
as the starless night
that holds me.

I see the face of days turned years
turned decades,
filling myself with food, drink, sedatives
somersaulting and drowning
in the truth.

I'm stuck.
I sit on the bench
of your court of love
and the verdict is guilty –
guilty for loving
guilty for staying.

I WAKE UP ALONE

We speak in whispers
where moonlight glows beneath.

Precious moments together,
wrapped up in time – defective time

always stops when it shouldn't.
Drops us into reality.

A reality where the air is still
and there's no trace of you.

Under moonlight,
we come back to this place
where I walk daily but don't recognize.

Without you it shows nothing.

In moonlight, it is a distant dream.
In moonlight, I breathe without you

with one-half a heartbeat.

I tingle under your gaze,
I shiver at your touch. You bring me back to life
from my empty existence.

Time's fleeting hands,
souls on fire – naked and vulnerable,
see each other as we are.
in moonlight: nothing withheld.

Part of me leaves with dawn.

I hold your hand in stillness
and wake up alone.

THE RESIDENCE
For D & J, who changed *everything*.

You've reached
the residence of

of these people
of these fools

you've reached
a bucket and barrel and passel of lies

you've reached
me
in my armor, ready for battle

you've reached
a machine
and a basket case
and a whore
they'll pretend to be normal but

don't believe them.

He's a shell and she's just desperate
for someone – something – to cling to
anyone or anything will do
that's how weak she is.

They're not your friends
they're your very worst enemies
straight outta grade school
a few years in college
and look, now we have something.

You've reached
real intelligence
groping towards nothing in particular
sex maybe –

silence
on the other end of the line

it was a mistake
but you pushed
so now you have it.
you've reached
me
I am victorious.

ACKNOWLEDGEMENTS

The Opera of Circumstance – first published in *Prism Galliard #10*, August 2000

Out & Through the Forgetting – first published in *Prism Galliard #10*, August 2000

Dissociation – first published in *Prism Galliard #10*, August 2000 as two separate poems: *Dissociation* and *Devastated*

Examination – first published in *Prism Galliard*, Volume V, Issue III Winter 2002

Permanence – first published in *Prism Galliard*, Volume V, Issue III Winter 2002

Crushed – first published in *Prism Galliard*, Volume V, Issue III Winter 2002

I Wake Up Alone – first published in *Prism Galliard*, Volume VI, Issue I Summer 2003

this is not a love poem – first published in *Blind Man's Rainbow #6*, April 2001

9147336R0

Made in the USA
Lexington, KY
01 April 2011